THE KINDNESS HABIT

5 STEPS TO MAXIMIZE
YOUR HAPPINESS AND IMPACT

ALLISON CLARKE, CSP

The Kindness Habit: 5 Steps to Maximize Your Happiness and Impact

Printed edition

©2018 Allison Clarke Consulting. All rights reserved.
First printing

For discounts on bulk purchases or to hire the author to speak to your organization, contact **allison@allisonclarkeconsulting.com**

P.O. Box 504
West Linn, Oregon 97068

ISBN: 978-0-9897330-2-1

Editors: Erin Donley, Christy Weber
Cover & Interior Design: Kee Rash

Printed in the United States of America

CONTENTS

Acknowledgments vii

Introduction xi

STEP 1
Stop during your daily routine 1

STEP 2
Look up and notice your surroundings. 11

STEP 3
Smile and take a deep breath 23

Photos 35

STEP 4
Appreciate one person each day 41

STEP 5
Remember your positive impact on others 55

25 Acts of kindness that celebrate human life: 65

Notes 67

About the author 75

ACKNOWLEDGMENTS

This book would not have happened without the talent of Erin Donley, thank you for working so hard with me over the years. Thank you to Christy Weber for your editing and Kee Rash for your design work.

Thank you to all the strangers who have made my day with your smile—opening my door, paying for my drink, letting me in the traffic line, helping with my bags, changing my tire, sending a kind message on social media, complimenting me, picking up trash, volunteering your time, saying "bless you" when I sneezed, and cheering me on at running events. You will never know how much I needed you that day.

Thank you to my dad for paying for my first Dale Carnegie class in 1994. That was the start of my career helping people solve communication problems and tap into their potential.

Thank you to my mom for teaching me the importance of writing thank you notes from the time I could write my name. Your focus on manners has shaped who I am today.

Aunt Anne, thank you for sending a card at EVERY holiday my entire life. Your kindness is felt by many.

Thank you to my clients, T2, friends, and family who have been so supportive of my journey as an entrepreneur. Kind fans like you keep me focused and motivated.

Thank you to the authors who provided quotes and research about kindness. You fill my brain with positive fuel daily. Keep writing!

Cheers to the next kind act we all can and will make happen.

"Act as if what you do makes a difference. It does."

– William James

INTRODUCTION

Has a stranger ever made your day?

When I ask that question to a room full of people, 90% raise their hands. They share memories of honor and recognition, and we linger for a moment in the feel-good effects of those unexpected deeds. It seems most of us have been on the receiving end of a random act of kindness. When it happens, it reminds us that mankind is inherently good and that we matter.

Then, I ask a question that elicits a different response, "If you know a stranger has the power to make you feel joyful, how often are *you* that person to someone else?"

The room gets quiet.

For over two decades, I've trained thousands of people how to express their appreciation for each other in the workplace. As one of Dale Carnegie's "Top 25 Master Trainers," I saw what could happen when people were acknowledged in their careers—their entire lives would transform. That's why this book exists today. Appreciating our fellow humans, I believe, is the ultimate pathway to happiness and success.

It's okay if you can't remember the last nice thing you did. Most of us are overwhelmed by to-do lists. Plus, technology encourages us to avoid live contact. It's become rare and even awkward to mingle with strangers, let alone with the ones we love. Because you've found your way to this book, however, you now have a chance to become an instrument of ongoing kindness. The Kindness Habit will get you in the flow of giving every single day.

Why bother? Former U.S. Senator Bob Kerrey perfectly explains, "Unexpected kindness is the most powerful, least costly, and most underrated agent of human change." [1] In the workplace, it can lower stress and skyrocket productivity. In the home, it can promote love and engagement. In your community, it can strengthen safety and make everyone feel like they belong.

Despite what's assumed, kindness isn't always taught in schools, nor is it properly modeled in all families, communities, media, or corporations. Yet, when a person demonstrates a dynamic sense of graciousness, it gets noticed and sparks a ripple effect of similar actions. I believe society is begging for ideas on how to be kind to each other. Knowing what's possible is half the battle. Putting thoughtfulness into motion is the fun and easy part.

The Kindness Habit offers five steps to follow each day. They are designed to bring forth your awareness and generosity for the people around you. Not only will strangers benefit, but so will everyone else in your life. Your new system of human recognition puts you in a position to give that doesn't deplete your resources. You get to tailor this process and choose *mutually* satisfying adventures.

Of course, there are obstacles to the Kindness Habit, but they're issues you already face—slowing down, putting away technology, exercising self-care, and considering the needs of others.

You might like a friend's post on social media and feel closer to them or skim an Instagram page and assume you know the person better. Don't let these superficial feelings of connection fool you. Online interaction pales in comparison to human touch, spoken words, and eye contact. My life and career, up until now, has proven this to be true.

In 1994, I joined the renowned company Dale Carnegie Training. My father offered to send me to their leadership program after his employee said it was the best thing he's ever done. So, I gave it a shot and was hooked. Their feedback form inquired, "How can we help you?" I asked if they had any employment openings.

Back then, I had a decent, but low-paying sales job, and on the weekends, I waitressed at Wankers Corner Saloon & Cafe, an iconic restaurant in Oregon. That's where I learned my best customer service. The owner created an inviting atmosphere where people wanted to come back continually. Remembering people's names, smiling, and having enthusiasm taught me how simple it was to make people feel important.

Dale Carnegie soon offered me a position in sales and training. Professionals flocked to our programs to better themselves in business. It was the first time I had been able to see what happens when a person's strengths were identified and spoken out loud. People would become enlivened, which led to marriages that were mended, families that were united, and friendships that were able to flourish. The ripple effect astounded me!

After training around the U.S., I'd drive home on the biggest natural high ever. Famous philosopher William James explained why, "The deepest craving in human nature is the craving to be appreciated." [2] Witnessing this in others filled me up in the same fashion. Their energy was contagious.

While honing my skills with Dale Carnegie, I had a bittersweet revelation. Their environment made me feel appreciated like never before. When others would say what made me unique and effective, I felt unstoppable in what I could accomplish. For the first time, I realized why some of my personal relationships had become painful—I didn't feel appreciated by those people.

By then, I had become a mother to my girls, Jenna and Jamie. My goal as a parent was to surround them with positive people who knew how to be encouraging. I needed that for myself, too. By then, I had evidence of how *rare* it was for people to feel truly valued.

After 16 years with Dale Carnegie Training, I launched my own company, Allison Clarke Consulting. The companies and organizations who hire me know success depends on their people. That's why we focus on the human side of business. Employee appreciation, communication, and leadership influence their bottom line, and they wouldn't dare ignore it.

Fred Meyer, a division of Kroger, was one of my first clients to concentrate on their associates. My first assignment was to help with the opening of a new store. Together, we improved all their systems—from the interview process and customer engagement to associate appreciation. We even did flash mobs in the store to inject fun into the grocery shopping experience. That location wound up receiving the highest score of engagement of all Kroger stores in the United States. This uplifted vibe was felt by everyone, including customers, and it caught *The Oregonian*'s attention. The newspaper named them one of the "Top Places to Work."[3]

Remember in kindergarten when you'd get a gold star on your paper? People love that at every age. Many have an unspoken longing to be singled out and celebrated. If their boss or coworkers don't make them feel special, they'll find a place that will. This is the number one reason people leave jobs. It's also the main reason people leave intimate relationships. We don't want to doubt that we're loved.

In 2011, peer pressure from other professional speakers compelled me to write a leadership book with an unusual twist. "What Will They Say? 30 Funerals in 60 Days" was published a year later. On a mission to learn what memories of us stay alive after we're dead, I attended 30 funerals of people whom I didn't know. This provided even more proof that life is about giving. Survivors of loss recalled one primary thing from the deceased—what that person had done for them.

In these sorrowful situations, humor lightened things up when it was needed most. At one service, a grieving daughter stood up and read funny letters from her father. It allowed everyone to sense this man's spirit, which was now eternal through his letters. The power of our words can live on through time.

Dedication was a big theme at funerals. It was touching when a 90-year-old, retired teacher talked about how the man who died never missed a parent-teacher conference for his stepdaughter. Loyalty is viewed as a tremendous kindness. We want to trust others to show up when we need them. The suicide funerals were the most heart-wrenching because the services always seemed to be packed. I'd sit there and wonder if they still would have taken their lives if they knew how many people treasured their existence. Writing the book about funerals upped my game in terms of creating urgency, appreciating people, being a good listener, and not having regrets. It especially reminded me that we all can make a difference.

I started to wonder why people were happy and charitable during the holiday season, but once the New Year rolled around, they shifted inward and became fixated on their resolutions. I questioned what it would take to sustain their desire to give, celebrate, and make others feel special. This caused me to start a 90-Day Kindness Challenge beginning on December 1st. Each day included a random act of kindness, along with a picture and description on my Facebook page. I hoped people would join me in keeping the holiday spirit alive through the month of February. If they could document how good it felt and have a reason to keep going post-holiday, maybe they wouldn't want to stop?

On the 50th day, HuffPost asked to write a story about the Kindness Challenge. They listed some of my random acts:

- Hung a wreath on a porta-potty
- Made certificates for "Best Parked Car"
- Gave a Power Ranger doll to a guy working out hard at the gym
- Left Pez® candy and a note for the mail carrier
- Found the "Best Smile in Portland" and gave him an award
- Bought white tulips for a woman sitting alone at a coffee shop
- Gave an eyeball toy to a 15-year-old who made good eye contact with adults

These acts made me laugh, and they helped me see the best in others.[4]

People's reactions always surprised me—hearty laughs, misty eyes, disbelief, and gushing appreciation. Sometimes, I heard about illness, death, divorce, and job loss. It reminded me how we have no idea what people are going through as they drive to work, shop for groceries, or rush through an airport. A favorite quote of mine from Plato says it best: "Be kind, for everyone you meet is fighting a hard battle."

Sometime after the HuffPost story, I heard from the corporate office of KIND® in New York. They heard about my 90-day Kindness Challenge and wanted to supply me with KIND bars to distribute around town and at all my keynotes. Rochelle, a local marketing person from their company, met with me, and since 2014, they've been sponsoring my daily acts and replenishing my community KIND bar stash.

When it comes to giving, you must discover your style. I like loading up on dollar store items, coming up with amusing awards, and writing messages on mirrors for my kids with dry-erase markers. If that's not your thing, you can buy coffee for the person behind you, leave a generous tip, or let someone in front of you during traffic. It can be as easy as leaving a sticky note in a bathroom saying, "Your life matters."

Three years later, the Kindness Challenge has continued well beyond 90 days. A reporter from a Portland TV station asked if anyone has ever denied me. In all this time, only one person said no. It was a busy construction worker who said, "You cannot take my picture, and I cannot take your prize." He was probably in the witness protection program, I joked.

It's worth noting: Some people are better at giving than receiving. Some don't like either. It doesn't matter. You are adopting the Kindness Habit to strengthen your own relationship with reciprocity. Your actions will demonstrate high-quality engagement, and you'll become a role model to younger generations who are losing social skills because they have their heads buried in screens.

Ideally, you'll want to practice the Kindness Habit everywhere you go, yet much can be done without leaving your home or neighborhood. For instance, I mailed handwritten letters this week, picked up trash in the street, and removed leaves from the drainage ditch. Small actions can become a big deal. Spotting the opportunities is key.

That's why I've developed a five-step process to make kindness a habit. It became important to teach this in my corporate trainings and keynotes, and to learn how anyone could make it work:

Step 1: Stop during your daily routine.

Step 2: Look up and notice your surroundings.

Step 3: Smile and take a deep breath.

Step 4: Appreciate one person each day.

Step 5: Remember your positive impact on others.

Everyone needs motivation in order to change their ways. People think money is the ultimate motivator, but when the website Delivering Happiness showcased author Daniel Pink, they listed his three vital factors that lead to positive and lasting growth: autonomy, mastery, and purpose. In his book, *Drive: The Surprising Truth about What Motivates Us*, Pink describes why self-direction (autonomy) results in higher satisfaction. If you can choose what actions to take on, ease and interest will naturally follow. With the Kindness Habit, autonomy can be achieved because you get to design how this practice looks for you.

Pink explains next how we yearn for progress (mastery). This helps us endure mundane and tedious tasks. The Kindness Habit gives mastery a chance because you have limitless opportunities to get creative and grow your generosity.

Pink says motivation occurs when there is a cause (purpose) that is larger than yourself. "Purpose is what gets you out of bed in the morning and into work without groaning or grumbling—something that you just can't fake." The Kindness Habit causes unexpected smiles and the opening of hearts. That alone can be your purpose, and you won't be disappointed.[5]

I was recently asked, "What's the kindest things anyone's ever done for you?" On Mother's Day, my daughters made a video with my friends, family, and clients saying what I meant to each of them. It was like being at my funeral, and I couldn't have been happier to attend. William James offers another simple truth, "Act as if what you do makes a difference. It does." [6] Thanks to my girls, I sobbed at the remembrance of this.

The Kindness Habit will support you in becoming a conduit of constant kindness. You don't have to have children, become successful, or get rich and famous to leave a noble legacy. Your good deeds are enough. Now's the time to show the world how it's done. Ready to make someone's day?

STOP DURING YOUR DAILY ROUTINE

Every day in the United States, nine people die and 1060 are hurt in car accidents caused by texting, operating navigation, eating, and using cell phones. That's one death every 2.6 hours due to multitasking. The U.S. ranks #1 internationally for distracted driving, and the number one killer of American teens is texting and driving.[1]

It's easy to soar through the day on autopilot and forget to check your pace. Busy is the norm, and we strive to make our days as productive as possible. Unless something goes wrong, we almost never question how we spend our time, or if we are present for any of it. Same is true with our thoughts. Scientists suggest we have roughly 70,000 thoughts per day.[2] Unless our words get us in trouble or our feelings cause discomfort, we may *never* question if those thoughts are harmful or healthy.

Here's an exercise to open your awareness:

Pretend there are hidden cameras filming you from the moment your eyes open in the morning. Before bed, you are given a review of what you thought, how you felt, and how you spent your time. This gives you a chance to witness yourself like never before.

How much worrying am I doing?

What kind of foods am I eating?

What judgments do I have?

How much time am I spending online?

How often do I show appreciation?

How many risks do I take?

How honest am I?

How often do I text and drive?

Where do I spend my money?

How often do I offer (or ask for) help?

You might not like what those hidden cameras revealed. You might feel embarrassed or ashamed and hope no one ever sees the footage. Don't let that stop you from reviewing yourself each day. Every worthy habit involves a little pain. This is a chance to privately uncover your blind spots. Instead of wanting to change because of defeat, you can choose to change for the sake of human kindness.

Inspirational advisor Ralph Marston said, "Give, not because it is an obligation, or because you've been guilted or shamed into doing so. Give because it is one of the greatest things you can do for yourself."[3]

The initial phase of the Kindness Habit requires you to slow down for a very intentional reason—you'll feel drained if you give to others without giving to yourself first. Discovering your most pressing needs takes vigilant inspection. This is how you pinpoint areas for better decision-making. Think about what those hidden cameras exposed.

What were your biggest time wasters?

What situations shook your confidence?

Which thoughts were damaging to your goals?

If you keep inquiring, you'll eventually refine your choices. First, you must take **Step 1: Stop during your daily routine.**

When I coach professionals, I gather confidential information from their managers, peers, and direct reports about their experiences with my client. After over 20 years of interviewing, assessments, and workshops, I've discovered that 70-90% of the respondents want two things: more appreciation and more feedback. This means we have to slow down in business and make time for other people.

Appreciation doesn't have to take hours. It can be a three-minute exercise. Schedule an "appreciation lap" each day in the office. Get up, leave your desk, walk around, make eye contact, and say hello to those you encounter—including parking lot attendants, groundskeepers, receptionists, or the cleaning crew. Send yourself a daily reminder or set an alarm to ensure this action occurs.

Acknowledging others might only take minutes, but giving thoughtful feedback deserves careful consideration. Finding words isn't the hardest part. The challenge is having to be present with yourself first. You must stop and merge with silence in order to sort through your feelings. This means you have to get quiet and get real before speaking. It's the kind thing to do before voicing your opinions, especially if they're about somebody else.

Author Maggie Jackson warns that performance goes down when we juggle too many tasks. "When you're multitasking, you're using a different neural network that relates to automatic behavior." She's saying that when you multitask, you won't be able to access higher thinking, so your words will lack insight, originality, and might be incorrect. Jackson demonstrates with a shocking statistic: "When doctors have ten minutes of reflection on a difficult case, it boosts diagnostic accuracy by 50%."[4]

Multitasking leads to errors. The military has found that when a soldier's brain was overloaded with information, it led to a host of unintended mistakes, like pulling the wrong lever or worst-case scenario, the loss of civilian lives.[5] When we multitask, the frontal lobe of the brain becomes taxed which weakens our ability to control impulses and make sound decisions.

In the book, *A Deadly Wandering*, author Matt Richtel introduces what he calls "the astonishing science of attention in the digital age." He mentions an experiment with undergraduate students who were asked to choose between a rich chocolate cake and a healthy fruit salad. To complicate their decision, some had to memorize a seven-digit number while others were give two digits only. In the end, chocolate cake became the popular choice for those with complicated numbers.[6]

Makes sense, don't you think? It explains why we make less than ideal selections when we are stressed, tired, hungry, or overwhelmed. But, you can free yourself from this domino effect of demands. See what it's like to expect less from yourself. You might actually accomplish more.

One thing your hidden cameras would show is how much time you give to technology. How often do you allow your smartphone to interrupt you? Who do you ignore when game requests, texts, or emails appear? What effect does this have on your relationship to them?

As the first radical act of kindness to yourself, turn off notifications from anyone or anything that isn't urgent. Who are the chosen few that you'll allow into your realm? Be selective! While you're at it, have designated times each day when you check your inbox. Let people know when you'll respond to emails, so you can manage their expectations. Set an autoresponder or verbally explain, "I only check email twice per day. If there's an emergency, call me."

With that said, I encourage my clients to have phone-free meetings. It ups the quality of connection and cuts meeting times in half. Some people like taking notes on their laptops and phones. That's fine, but what happens when a text arrives or you get a Facebook notification? You might not open it, but it still interrupts your attention. Knowing that your brainpower is being compromised should motivate you to track your notes another way.

You've probably heard that technology affects sleep quality. The National Sleep Foundation reports, "Blue screens on cell phones, computers, tablets, and televisions restrain the production of melatonin, which makes it harder to fall and stay asleep." They say to put away technology at least 30 minutes before bedtime and keep electronics out of the bedroom.[7] Getting adequate rest is as important as food, exercise, and oxygen. It's also a fundamental act of self-kindness, especially as you age. Give yourself this space to restore.

If you're sleeping better at night, why not get up earlier, too? The most successful people I know have one similar trait— the get up before sunrise and exercise. According to former U.S. Navy SEAL commander Jocko Willink, "one of the most common ways sabotage your morning [is] to gradually wake up over projects that require thinking."[8] Instead, get moving. Start with an energizing accomplishment.

Another way to prepare for success is to make your bed, as soon as your feet hit the floor. In the book, *Make Your Bed:*

Little Things That Can Change Your Life . . . And Maybe the World, Admiral William H. McRaven calls this two-minute chore, "simple and mundane," yet he says, "it can you help maintain a sense of discipline throughout the day."[9] There's also an aesthetic payoff. When you see smooth covers, you can visualize a smooth day ahead. And at night, you'll get to crawl into a tidy bed that's ready to embrace you.

You'll also want to schedule Zen into your day. Surely, those hidden cameras recorded the pile of clothes on your treadmill, your unused journals, or books you have yet to read on your nightstand. Set aside at least 20 minutes a day for self-care. This could be a creative project, a karaoke party, yoga class, or a comedy on Netflix. You define what Zen means to you.

Swedish company, Skanska Construction, makes this a business practice. They spend ten minutes every morning as a team doing "Stretch & Flex." This is where they review project details and physically stretch. This routine helps them get on the same page, but more than anything, it ensures their safety. I'll never forget stretching with 1000 workers at one of their sites.

Zen has found its way into boardrooms as well. Corporate mindfulness teaches how to track your emotions, so you won't react to stress. This helps you plan your next moves with discernment. Mindfulness has calmed nerves on Wall Street, yet it has a downside, too. Buddhist monk Matthieu Ricard cautions that corporate mindfulness does good, but it doesn't necessarily make you good. He says it can turn into "me me me" mindfulness.[10] That's why I'm passionate about the Kindness Habit. You get to slow down, become aware, and provide self-care. Then, your attention will move on to everyone else.

Another surprising discovery from my career in corporate training—confidence is lacking in the workplace. It's human nature to compare, worry, and fixate on your flaws. When these thoughts arise, make sure you write them down. Let yourself see the words that swirl through your mind, so you can properly challenge their truth and remove them.

How would you rewrite your fears to make them positive?
What would it take to believe the new version?
Can negativity prompt you to give and be kind?

When I coach teams on how to give better presentations, they write down all the reasons they're going to do well, "I'm an expert in my field, my words have value, I care about the audience, and I want them to learn." This exercise psyches up the brain and helps you see the best in yourself. Then, you start seeing the best in others. The transition has to start with you. Lao Tzu said, "Kindness in words creates confidence. Kindness in thinking creates profoundness. Kindness in giving creates love."

If you need a place to begin your Kindness Habit, I recommend starting at work. We spend the majority of the week at our jobs. Make it your practice ground for kindness. This will give you confidence to give back in creative and loving ways to your family, friends, and strangers. Your success with one group will feed another.

Here are a few ways to practice kindness at work:

- Take a new person out to lunch
- Hold doors for coworkers
- Take time to mentor
- Change empty toilet paper rolls

- Bring treats for everyone to share
- Tell Sally she has spinach in her teeth
- Buy coffee for a coworker
- Surprise someone with flowers
- Celebrate people's milestones
- Listen if someone is hurting or sad
- Put away your phone in meetings
- Write a glowing testimonial for a client
- Live your company's core values

I've always liked the phrase, "You are your own billboard." Once, I saw a client act rude to a hotel clerk, which shed light on his character. If hidden cameras were rolling, he wouldn't have wanted that to be seen. Actually, there might have been *real* cameras filming. Video rolls continuously at grocery stores, casinos, airports, and gas stations. Screenshots can be captured as evidence. And does anyone else besides me get secretly filmed by their kids? There's always someone who can see you. Don't forget that.

Sports Business Radio host, Brian Berger, trains high-profile athletes how to converse with the media. His motto is "You're always on record. Everything is permanent." What is your billboard saying when you're in the house, exiting your car, or speaking publicly to anyone? You are no longer invisible. Your words and actions will be noted by someone. Look at how many people have been fired because of their social media posts and from people recording their missteps. Wouldn't you rather be noted for your kindness on and offline?

Defensive end for the Houston Texans J.J. Watt recently made history off the field. He was named *Sports Illustrated*'s

2017 "Sportsperson of the Year" because of his goal to raise $200,000 for Hurricane Harvey relief in Houston. In the end, he raised more than $37 million. He didn't anticipate the windfall of donations, and his efforts showed the world what one man's kindness has the power to do.[11]

Consider this: How you return a shopping cart at the grocery store says a lot about you. Do you leave it in the middle of the parking lot? Do you bring it back, but it's sticking out sideways? Do you push it together neatly with the other carts? It's kind to put things back where they belong. Order is appreciated by all, and who knows who may be watching to see if you took the extra step?

The Kindness Habit begins by questioning your patterns, slowing down, and inserting breaks in your daily routine. This gives you space to honor yourself and consider where else you may be needed. This pause in the day prepares you for Step 2, which became apparent to me while traveling for business.

When boarding airplanes, I notice elderly people struggling with their luggage. Sitting next to them is a passenger who doesn't even realize they are needed because they are looking down at their phone. I want to scream, "Hey, look up for a second!" That's what needs to happen next for kindness to occur.

Now that you're primed to **stop during your daily routine**, let's see what the world has to offer when you look up and take in your surroundings.

STEP 2

LOOK UP AND NOTICE YOUR SURROUNDINGS

I've learned there's a *genuine* reason we stare at our phones in public: When personal space is invaded, it's a coping mechanism to put your head down and avoid eye contact. You'll notice this on elevators, on public transportation, and in grocery store lines. Diverting your eyes helps manage insecurity and avoid uncomfortable situations. It fails, however, at inspiring kind deeds.

There's a time and place for zoning out with technology. You might feel exhausted or under the weather, or maybe you're in a state of emotional grief. Smartphone therapy could be the remedy you need. Our screens are a safe haven. Our information and schedules live there, and we're known, on some level, by people online. Technology can offer comfort and relief, though, but be sure to remember two key points: There are healthier ways to self-medicate, and you always have a choice.

The Kindness Habit, Step 1, encouraged you to stop during your daily routine. This gave you insights into what you've been doing with your time. When you saw what thoughts or behaviors weren't aligned with your goals, you made adjustments to serve your greater good. Congratulations!

Step 2 invites you to **look up and notice your surroundings**. This is your new playground of wonder and compassion, and in this chapter, you'll get to see the possibilities available to you there. You have to look up to discover who needs your help.

This step might seem fussy. Do you really need a reminder to look up? Yes! There's a deliberate reason for this "stop, drop, roll" tempo. If you were given a list of 100 random acts of kindness, you'd probably carry out a few, but to make kindness a habit, your brain needs to identify the specific steps involved. That's how it sets a new pattern in place.

In 2006, researchers at Duke University estimated that 40% of our daily actions are not conscious decisions. They are habits performed on autopilot. In the book, *The Power of Habit*, author Charles Duhigg says, "This process—in which the brain converts a sequence of actions into an automatic routine—is known as 'chunking,' and it's the root of how habits form." He continues, "Habits, scientists say, emerge because the brain is constantly looking for ways to save effort."[1] Take your morning routine, for example. You don't have to think very hard to make coffee, take a shower, and drive to work. When the brain starts to recognize a habit, it shifts into autopilot because it's always aiming for efficiency. This gives your mind a chance to relax or focus elsewhere.

Have you ever driven somewhere and didn't remember being on the road? It's scary when that happens. It means the brain has registered the steps and engrained the habit. Could this be why we think it's okay to play with the phone while driving? It can seem like we're managing just fine, yet in this multitasking attempt, lives are at stake, and the road ahead is truly all that matters.

"Being present" is an abstract concept for most Americans. I describe it as focusing on the task or person in front of you without thinking about the past or future. Mastering presence can seem unreasonable when there are deadlines at work, bills to pay, kids to pick up, and a dog who needs two walks per day. "Being in the now" doesn't mean you abandon these obligations. It means you show up completely when you're there.

Spiritual teacher Eckhart Tolle said, "Stress is caused by being here, but wanting to be there, or being in the present, but wanting to be in the future. It's a split that tears you apart inside."[2]

This means when you walk the dog, you'll want to smell the flowers, look up at the sky, touch the leaves, listen to the birds, and send love to your furry friend. It means when you work on financial spreadsheets, you'll want to power down your phone, close your office door, ask for quiet time, and start the task by giving thanks for your income and occupation.

Harvard University researched why social media is addictive—because humans love to disclose information about themselves. An MRI showed that when people post their views and photos online, pleasure regions light up in the brain, as if they had been "eating, receiving money or having sex."[3] I can see how social media sharing can be gratifying, but it seems like pleasure comes mostly from validation, which can sometimes be hundreds and thousands of people saying they approve. For many, this becomes a drug!

Since validation seems readily available online, isn't it fascinating that appreciation and feedback are the top requests from professionals at work? You'd think Facebook alone could satisfy those needs. I think it's clear what's happening—we, as a society, are starving for in person, human connection. We want to be seen, heard, and acknowledged by those around us.

Filmmaker Prince Ea rapped about social media fatigue in his viral, YouTube video, "Can We Auto-Correct Humanity?" He said, "I'm so tired of performing in a pageantry of vanity and conforming to this digital insanity."[4] His words resonate with millions who are ready to reclaim their time and self-worth. The point isn't to unplug completely, but rather to balance your involvement with digital devices.

Instead of viewing Step 2 as a demand to remove technology, see it as a call to get curious about your environment. Commit to finding something new each day, and you'll reap the benefits of engaging with your environment, rather than technology. The rewards have no limits.

To instill Step 2 into your everyday actions, here are a few benefits that occur when you **look up and notice your surroundings:**

- Gain a competitive edge in business: Knowing when to put technology away speaks volumes about your professionalism. While everyone is distracted and looking down, you will stand out as the one who is making eye contact.

- New research indicates that even the presence of a cell phone in meetings can lessen the quality of conversation. Why take that risk with business? Show others that you know how to be present and give them the respect they deserve.

  KINDNESS CHALLENGE: Write down what situations (or people) cause you to look down at your phone. Who are you trying to avoid? What do you fear will happen? What skills do you need to be confident?

- **Get healthy and happy with nature**: Billions of dollars are spent each year in healthcare, and yet outside the door is Mother Earth, a continuous resource that energizes and soothes. Reports show that being in nature improves concentration, lessens feelings of anger, boosts immunity, reduces stress, and improves your mood.

- In a study, environmental writer Naima Montacer talks about nature's powerful effects on the body, mind, and spirit. Regarding a hospital study, she said, "Patients with a tree to view through their window had shorter hospital stays, received fewer negative comments from nurses, took fewer analgesics, and had slightly lower scores for post-surgical complications." Schools with nature programs have reported higher test scores, graduation rates, and numbers of students who are interested in college.[5] There's no doubt about it, we are meant to merge with nature.

  KINDNESS CHALLENGE: Find an outdoor hobby for each season. If you don't want to do it alone, find a group or partner who will keep you accountable and engaged.

- **Enliven your senses like never before:** When you look up, your sights will instantly register what's nearby. This will heighten your hearing, taste, smell, and touch. For instance, if you turn off the TV during dinner, you're likely to eat more slowly, notice all the flavors, and relish each bite of your meal, which could even help with digestion.

  I once attended the Blind Cafe, which is a music, poetry, and dinner event in pitch-black darkness.

When I entered the room, my senses went into overdrive. Without being able to perceive my food, company, or even my own hand, I spent the evening more quiet than usual. My senses were intensely robust, and it caused me to appreciate every voice that spoke and every morsel I ate.

KINDNESS CHALLENGE: Go outside during your breaks at work. Even if the weather is extreme, immerse yourself in nature for a few minutes every day. Silently, take note of what you see, hear, taste, smell, and feel. This is mindfulness in motion!

- **Increase your chances for safety:** It's common to hear stories about pedestrians getting hit because they were staring at their phones while walking or their headphones prevented them from hearing. This also causes them to bump into people, crash into poles, trip on curbs, and damage expensive property because they had zero awareness. People even fall off cliffs and trip down stadium stairs, all in pursuit of the perfect selfie!

When an automatic habit, such as walking and driving, is combined with multitasking, the consequences can be tragic. The NHTSA said texting and driving is equivalent to driving with a blood alcohol level three times the legal limit.[6] Think about how devastated and embarrassed you'd be if your "must send" text was the cause of a deadly occurrence.

KINDNESS CHALLENGE: If you must use your smartphone while driving, find a safe place to pull over. Now that you've read the dangers of distracted driving, stop immediately, as a kindness to yourself and humanity.

- **Build stronger unions with those you love:** You can be in the same physical space as others and be checked-out emotionally with technology. This is a form of neglect and a missed opportunity for intimacy. According to nurse, author, and TEDx speaker Maureen McGrath, "10% of people check their phones during sex and 35% check them immediately afterwards."[7] Those statistics left her audience aghast!

When you come home from work, do you relax with your newsfeed and news apps? Give yourself 10 minutes to unwind online, then get reacquainted with your most precious people. You've probably seen families and couples not talking at a restaurant because they're all on their devices. Lack of eye contact is generally interpreted as lack of caring.

KINDNESS CHALLENGE: If you're engaged with technology and a person speaks to you, turn it off or set it down before answering them. This is your chance to demonstrate a kind courtesy which is needed now, more than ever.

- **Become a better listener:** Hearing is the experience of receiving sound waves, while listening requires your participation. You cannot listen and look at your devices simultaneously, and you can't effectively communicate if both parties aren't involved. In Stephen R. Covey's book, *The 7 Habits of Highly Effective People*, he names The Five Levels of Listening

LEVEL 1: Ignoring – not listening or hearing at all

LEVEL 2: Pretending – looks like listening, but the mind is elsewhere

LEVEL 3: Selective Listening – hearing only certain parts of the conversation

LEVEL 4: Attentive Listening – paying attention and focusing energy on the words being spoken

LEVEL 5: Empathetic Listening – using empathy and intent to understand, get inside the speaker's frame of reference, and see the world as they see it[8]

KINDNESS CHALLENGE: At what level do you listen to others? Place a number from Covey's Five Levels of Listening next to each group or person. Notice who gets level 4-5 attention and who receives 1-3. Why do some get preferential treatment?

_____ Family		_____ Friends	
_____ Team Members		_____ Customers	
_____ Partners		_____ Children	
_____ Community Members		_____ Strangers	
_____ Service Workers		_____ Boss	

- **Don't stress out in traffic:** When drive times are delayed, these interruptions can add issues and insanity. Next time your car comes to an unexpected halt, see it as a call to awaken your inner Buddha and practice patience.

In Portland, Oregon, traffic times keep getting longer each year. That's why I created an automotive self-care strategy. Whether I'm stuck on a highway or stopped by a passing train, my meditative plan keeps me calm and prepared.

KINDNESS CHALLENGE: Read these tips and practice them next time you're stranded on the road.

AC's 7 Tips for Traffic Sanity & Safety:

1. Make sure you have enough gas in your tank. If you get stuck, you'll be safe and warm for hours.

2. Keep bottled water and snacks on hand. Having an empty stomach can make the extended commute seem like forever.

3. Have a phone charger handy. You'll relax if you can let others know where you are, why you're delayed, and when they can expect you. This is also a great time to catch up with friends—on your hands-free device, of course!

4. Keep your mind amused and educated with podcasts, talk shows, audio books, or music. *Throwback Jams* always get me singing and dancing. Other times, I choose symphony music to unwind.

5. Look for entertainment in people's bumper stickers and license plates. Read billboards, discover new businesses, gaze at the trees, and get curious about the debris on the side of the road. While you're at it, check out people in cars around you. Remember, they're watching you, too!

6. If there's an accident, consider those who are involved and send supportive thoughts to everyone, including EMTs and police on the scene. You might be 15 minutes late, but that's nothing compared to those in the wreck.

7. Take a few deep breaths. (More on this topic in Step 3) If the weather permits, roll down your window and get some fresh air. Keep some lavender oil in the car. Dab a few drops on your wrist or sniff from the bottle for quick relaxation.

- **Discover the good in each person, place, or thing:** When you **look up and notice your surroundings**, do it with the intention of finding what's positive. I practice this intent when handing out made-up awards, like Best Parking or Greatest Smile.

  Next time you're in line at the store, find what's appealing or clever about the building, displays, or the clerk who's about the help you. If you see trash on the floor, pick it up. If you see a person crying, hand them a tissue. Do something to make each situation a little better.

  KINDNESS CHALLENGE: Take notice of the color of people's eyes. I find you can always see what's good in a person after you've looked into what's called "the window of the soul." Eye contact can increase likeability and trust and can quiet your negative judgments.

By now, you can see how looking up and observing are becoming rare acts. Would you like to be an exception? Step 2 of the Kindness Habit positions you to become a role model for presence, optimism, and connection. While others divert their eyes as a poor form of communication, you'll offer the gift of your attention, which French philosopher Simone Weil called "the rarest and purest form of generosity."[9]

It's understandable that we're tied to our smartphones. They've replaced our calendars, alarms, flashlights, calculators, dictionaries, cameras, newspapers, and more. The trick is to manage your time with technology, set boundaries, and don't trick yourself into believing that device is better than live humans for conversation and companionship.

British filmmaker Gary Turk released a touching video called "Look Up." He speaks about our collective addiction to devices and their isolating effects. His message has enlightened millions of viewers and created a social movement. "So when you're in public, and you start to feel alone, put your hands behind your head, and step away from the phone. You don't need to stare at your menu or contact list. Just talk to one another. Learn to coexist."[10]

SMILE AND TAKE A DEEP BREATH

One thing I love about the holidays is the way it makes people smile and act generous. We wear funny Christmas sweaters to instigate laughs, we deliver cookies to neighbors and friends, and we send meaningful cards to those who have made a difference. In December, we're more likely to say hello to a stranger, but as soon as the New Year hits, people become self-focused. This contrast in kindness never ceases to amaze me!

In 2014, I started a 90-Day Kindness Challenge that began December 1st. I hoped people would see my random acts of kindness that were posted on Facebook and want to join me through February to keep the holiday spirit alive, if even only with their smile. One day, I put together a basket of snacks for delivery workers and left it by my front door. During the holidays, these dedicated folks carry their heaviest loads and push themselves through long hours. In my basket, I included KIND bars for fuel and bottled water for hydration, and I posted a picture of it online. In most cases, I didn't get to see the drivers' reactions, but sometimes, they left me a note of thanks or waved from their truck. This idea was inspired from a social media post that I modified in my own way.

The basket idea wound up taking off online. People nationwide put together their own baskets and posted their photos. No doubt, this made the workers smile, and it made me feel elated to see a kindness that can be done any time of year. Think about how those drivers' moods may have changed after receiving appreciation. It might have helped them get through their shift, so they could show up at home with more energy for their family. It's fun to think about the chain reaction you can start with one act of kindness.

Step 1: Stop during your daily routine.
Stop what you're doing when a delivery vehicle arrives.

Step 2: Look up and notice your surroundings.
Look up and notice the energy and effort they put into their jobs.

Step 3: Smile and take a deep breath.
Smile and take a deep breath to become fully present.

You have reached the final inner preparation that's needed to carry out a kind deed. Like Steps 1 and 2, the third step is meant to enliven your body and brain, so you can place your attention on others with *sincere* joy.

Before you proceed, I have to warn you—when you look up, make eye contact, and flash a good-natured smile, people might think you're crazy. I saw a meme that describes this sign-of-the-times embarrassment: "Being polite is so rare these days it's often confused with flirting."

When you gift a stranger with a smile, you will be viewed as unique and maybe even puzzling because a) you weren't looking down at your phone in public and most people are and b) your smile provided an unexpected rush of delight, which tends to throw people for a loop! Nevertheless, you must proceed. Mother Teresa said, *"We shall never know all the good that a simple smile can do.*"[1] Plus, it's easy, free, and possible for everyone.

Has a stranger ever made your day with their smile? Of course, they have. It's a thrill to be on the giving *and* receiving end of a silent hello. Poet Rainier Maria Rilke paints a beautiful picture of this interaction: "Sometimes to someone lonely there comes something that works as a wondrous balm. It's not a sound, not even a voice. It is the smile of a woman—a smile, that, like the light of perished stars, is still on its way."[2]

Your smile is force of nature, regardless of gender and age. It's capable of regulating your heartbeat and energizing your brain. It has the same effect on those who receive your smile. In this chapter, I'll explain what science tells us about smiles and deep breathing, and I'll share as a corporate coach what training thousands of people has taught me about the absolute necessity of a smile in business.

As a kid, I loved waving to strangers from the back of the school bus in Evergreen, Colorado. Did you do that, too? When they'd wave back and smile, we would cheer like crazy and think we were cool. We learned early in life that a smile equals a reward. Statistics imply that children smile an average of 400 times per day, while adults smile around 20 times per day, and if they're happy, it's 40-50.[3] In business, however, smiling is essential to success, so it has to be practiced and even coerced at times.

Kelton Research has reported, "Job applicants who smiled during an interview were 58% more likely to be hired, and their salaries were 53% larger."[4] In sales training, it's standard advice to smile when talking on the phone. Why? Because your tone of voice is capable of putting people at ease and gaining their trust. When your lips are upturned, you can't help but sound upbeat. Even if you're the bearer of bad news, it won't sound as harsh when done with a smile. Try it sometime. It's nearly impossible to come across as mean or depressing when your lips are saying otherwise. Smiling is key to likeability in sales.

Having spent most of my career in front of large groups, I rarely get nervous before speaking. There's one exception, though—when the audience is full of my peers. I served as Oregon President of the National Speaking Association and have continued in leadership at NSA. This puts me in front of the country's most dynamic speakers, and I strive to be one of them! How do I find relief? Smiling.

Fellow speaker Darryl Davis researched nearly every aspect of a smile in his book, *How to Design a Life Worth Smiling About*. He explains there are four feel-good chemicals released when we smile. He uses a cleaver acronym to make them memorable: DOSE™: Dopamine, Oxytocin, Serotonin, and Endorphins.

DOPAMINE: People who are motivated and outgoing tend to thrive on dopamine because, as Davis explains, "it lets you know that either you are about to get something that you need or you are nearing a goal." Addictive drugs, such as cocaine, target the brain's dopamine receptors. This is what keeps users amped and wanting more.

OXYTOCINE: Davis calls it "The Love Chemical" because it causes us to be generous and to want to relate. Oxytocin is released when there is a "perceived type of bonding, such as your comment being 'liked' on a social media network." Davis says, "To help you remember what Oxytocin is, think of the *o* as meaning 'Others'."

SEROTONIN: This chemical gets activated when we're in the spotlight or receiving admiration. Davis tells us, "Serotonin is associated with our ability to deal with group dynamics and competition." He equates the two as "Serotonin=Status" and gives us the image of an alpha dog who is confidently leading the pack.

ENDORPHINS: According to Davis, "Endorphins=Energy." They are the chemicals that are responsible for what we call a "runner's high," which is our body's natural way to mask pain. When faced with an emotionally or physically unpleasant situation, your smile can have an opiate effect, which helps you get started and make it through.[5]

Armed with this information, I've made myself grin and bear it in times of struggle and uncertainty. A forced smile has given me the guts to bungee jump out of a hot air balloon, climb through Congo caves in South Africa, run a marathon, and start life over in seven states. As a parent, I've smiled my way through difficult decisions. As a speaker, my smile boosts my energy and helps me connect with all my audiences.

For some, the idea of "fake it 'til you make it" might seem inauthentic. Fair enough. It's important to honor your emotions. Find a time and place to be with people who support you. Your closest contacts don't need you to be chipper all the time, yet in public and at work, I believe our presence and positivity are required. That's why some people stand out as leaders. They know how to manage the energy they exude.

This doesn't mean you should pretend like everything's okay after a tragic event. It means you can get through a rough day by taking a deep breath, lighting up your eyes, and raising the corners of your mouth. People will be softer with you because you've been soft with them. Who knows where they have been before meeting you—a funeral, hospital, or a chaotic situation at home?

Going to work when you're angry or down might seem grueling, but people often say it gives them a break from those feelings. With each smile, your brain gets a chemical cocktail that makes it possible for you to focus on others, instead of yourself, and complete necessary tasks. It's not a cure-all for everything, but smiling can lessen your time of agony or grief.

Disney trains every employee, from baristas and groundskeepers to characters, to make the guests' enjoyment their top priority. Work time is considered "show time," and smiles and good moods are part of the Disney brand. Same thing happens at the Ritz Carlton. Employees view their jobs as a performance in customer service that aims for five stars with their ladies and gentlemen. This showbiz mentality, despite your industry, will guarantee smiles from each person on the team.

When I train professionals on their presentation skills, everyone gets filmed, so they can see themselves in action. Most people feel shocked when they see their footage. They had no idea they waved their hands, swayed back and forth, or tilted their head a certain way. Seeing their own mannerisms sets immediate change into motion, and their most common revelation is . . . they can't believe how *little* they were smiling!

First impressions get formed in just seven seconds. When you lead with a smile, it ups your chances of being liked and heard. Validation isn't the best part. Your smile will allow people to gain value from your words. Step 3 safeguards your message, so it can be received in the kindest and most receptive way possible.

Plus, smiling is infectious and so is laughter. We mimic people's speech patterns, movements, and attitudes without even realizing it. That's why frowning is contagious and so is negativity. "Mirroring" is a way to get comfortable in social situations and match people's moods, so there's a better chance that we'll click.

When you're speaking, do you know what your face is doing? This is another eye-opener for those who have never been filmed—they realize their resting face is either scowling or perplexed. This is why companies encourage mirrors in breakrooms and cubicles. You can practice having your face match your words and the appropriateness of a situation.

Harvard Business Review reports face-to-face requests are 34% more effective than email. Seeing a person's demeanor gives us information about them. That's why in business, there's a need to minimize phone and conference calls. Zoom, Skype, or Facetime allow people to read body language and show that they are listening. These video platforms are preferred because, above all, we cannot multitask when we're being watched.[6]

In the book, *Gestures, the Do's and Taboos of Body Language Around the World,* the author mentions the incredible discoveries of a researcher in kinesics, which is the study of body motion. Ray Birdwhistell estimates the face is able to make a whopping 250,000 expressions. Each of these play a role in aiding human connection.[7]

When faces aren't available, we rely on emojis to convey how we feel. If a written statement could be interpreted as combative, a happy face can show it was meant kindly. A winky face can imply sarcasm or playfulness, and a blushing smiley face will confirm a person's humility. With just one symbol, greater understanding can occur. It's no wonder we constantly add them for color and clarification.

Emojis have become so popular, they're sold as keychains, stickers, comforters, and decorative pillows. There's even a movie about emoji adventures! In 2015, *The Oxford English Dictionary* named "emoji" Word of the Year. There are about 100 facial emojis. That seems like a lot, but it's only a fraction of what the human face is capable of expressing. Perhaps our rampant use of emojis indicates how much we are craving real, live faces.

Have you ever sent a text or an email and it was taken the wrong way? That's because your body language and tone of voice were missing.

Choosing facial emojis over human interaction will make us increasingly lazy and weak. We won't have the challenge of finding words to express ourselves, and what will happen to our facial muscles? Darryl Davis says, "It takes 6 muscles to frown; 10 muscles are needed for a forced smile; and an authentic smile uses 12 or more."[8] With emojis, there are no muscles needed, but communication comes at a higher risk, and your facial muscles can't help but decline. So, think of smiling as a natural facelift.

Step 3: Smile and take a deep breath is meant put you in the best state of mind possible before you give to others. It's also another way to become informed about your overall demeanor, which includes your posture.

You can't take a proper, deep breath when you're slouched over your screen. Social psychologist Amy Cuddy says this position is detrimental to our bodies because when we lean forward 60 degrees or more, our necks are forced to support the additional 10 to 12 pounds that our heads weigh. This increases strain on the neck to a massive 60 pounds. There's a nickname for this chronic issue that's become prevalent with teens. It's called "iHunch."[9]

My chiropractor sees this as an ever-increasing problem. That's why he teaches patients to retrain how they sit and stand. Using Brugger's Posture Exercises, I've learned how to lift my head, straighten my back, pivot my shoulders, elevate my chest, and slant my lower torso forward. This provides space for my organs to do their job, and it opens my airwaves for cleansing deep breaths.

Your breath is a part of the Kindness Habit simply because it's what keeps you alive. It's a reminder that it's a miracle to wake up and be given another day. Breath is the gateway to our human experience. Life begins and ends with a breath, and children enter the world through the power of their mothers' breath. It deserves our daily reverence!

William Saroyan speaks about breath with passion and irreverence: "Try to learn to breathe deeply, really to taste food when you eat, and when you sleep, really to sleep. Try as much as possible to be wholly alive with all your might, and when you laugh, laugh like hell. And when you get angry, get good and angry. Try to be alive. You will be dead soon enough."[10]

As a speaker, I tap into my breath to get centered and calm, and it benefits my audience, too. An intentional pause, followed by an audible or visible deep breath, gives people a chance to absorb what they just heard. This is a form of kindness that every presenter should strive to provide. Your tempered breathing gives people time to apply the message to their own lives.

A cleansing breath comes from the belly, not the chest. Put your hand on your abdomen and have your air come from that area. If your hand doesn't rise and fall, it means you're chest breathing. Bring the energy down into your body. This is what it takes to get grounded and become present.

At the doctor, you've probably been told to take a deep breath. They tell us to breathe through discomfort because it actually works. You don't have to think to breathe, but when it's done mindfully, it can help you fight stress, lower blood pressure, boost immunity, and relax the body and mind.

This is why I'm such a big fan of essential oils. These natural scents cause us to take long and slow breaths. That's one of the ways we feel their effects. Lavender's Latin name is "lavare," which means "to wash." With each inhalation, it enhances circulation, soothes respiratory issues, relieves tension, and calms your nervous system. It even has disinfecting qualities on the scalp and skin.

I'm not the only lavender enthusiast, a university hospital in San Diego implemented a pilot project called Code Lavender. It was designed to increase acts of kindness after stressful workplace events occur. Code Lavender kits include handwritten words of comfort from a person in hospital management, a piece of chocolate, a vial of lavender oil, and employee health referral information, such as free psychological counseling.

Code Lavender was created because healthcare can be traumatizing, and there's a need for that to be acknowledged by those in the field. When a medical professional is offered a

Code Lavender kit, it recognizes what they've been through, gives them resources for healing, and it lets them know, they're not alone.[11] Wouldn't it be terrific if every business and home had this kindness kit available?

What would you put in *your* emotional first aid box?

As adults, we can teach younger generations the significance of controlled breathing. When faced with school stress, peer pressure, or an invitation to use drugs or alcohol, a young person can use a deep breath to help manage anxiety and find confidence to say no. Our children won't know how to do this themselves unless we show them when to apply it and how it's done.

I hope you've been able to grasp the potency of your smile and the potential of intentional breath. Their life-giving properties are within your control, even when they seem difficult to access. In Step 4, you'll learn how to view what's positive about whatever's in your field and give back to those who paint your daily landscape.

Until then, here are a few kind things you can do for yourself. These are meant to make you smile and give you fuel, so you'll have more energy to keep spreading kindness.

- Eat a delicious meal
- Hydrate with water
- Change your sheets
- Be on time
- Remember someone's name
- Get a new haircut
- Read a funny bumper sticker

- Hug someone
- Finish tasks in the yard
- Clean your car
- Go to a comedy club
- Leave a big tip
- Breathe fresh air
- Exercise outside
- Notice the cleanliness of a store
- Play with kids
- Listen to an elder
- Walk the dog
- Let the sun hit your face
- Pet an animal
- Watch live sports
- Buy fresh flowers
- Scream on roller coasters
- Pick up the phone and call someone who's been on your mind
- Visit an old friend
- Start a creative project
- Write a gratitude list
- Breathe from your core

I found this truck in a parking lot and left a "Best Truck" trophy on the hood. I didn't get to see the reaction, and I hope it made them smile.

I took time to tape a note and a few dollars on a vending machine at the local hospital. Think of environments that really need more kindness.

I had fun making this award and finding a car well parked in Portland, OR.

I left this toy for our waiter at a restaurant, plus a 20% tip for his awesome service. Make people smile with a fun surprise.

When you see trash on the ground, pick it up. On this day, I went to the local middle school with a trash bag to make a small difference.

I learned when training hotel employees in Reno, NV, that you should tip the housekeeping crew $2-3 per night. I always leave a note of thanks, cash, and sometimes a treat.

Here is the goodie basket I talked about on page 23. It felt great to offer fuel and nourishment during the long holiday hours.

I saw an expired parking meter and put in a quarter to save the person a ticket. Look up and around you for opportunities to be kind.

This is Rochelle Dobson, a Field Marketing Manager from KIND®. She is the one who heard about my kind acts, asked me to coffee, and gave me all sorts of fun, KIND products to share.

APPRECIATE ONE PERSON EACH DAY

When people feel appreciated at work, it makes them happy. That makes them 43% more productive, 86% more creative, and 51% less likely to leave.

These percentages are reported from Hay Group, Forbes, and UC Berkeley, yet *many* research teams have discovered this irrefutable truth—people thrive when they know their presence and contributions matter.[1] It's often life changing for them.

Step 4 of the Kindness Habit invites you to appreciate one person each day. In the previous steps, you've been able to boost your inner resources.

- Step 1, you became mindful of your daily routine.
- Step 2, you looked up and noticed the splendor that's around you.
- Step 3, you smiled and fueled your body with breath.

It's now time to engage your fellow human. Step 4 is where my professional expertise resides. I've trained thousands of leaders and worked with companies like Kroger, Intel, Trident Seafoods, Adidas, Transamerica, and Niagara Bottling to solve communication problems and reinforce the power of appreciation.

When I started Allison Clarke Consulting, I had been with Dale Carnegie for sixteen years and was one of their "Top 25 Master Trainers." My foundation for learning the impact of kindness came from Mr. Carnegie's Principle 2: "Give honest, sincere appreciation."[2]

When this rule was practiced, I'd watch people from all walks of life nearly fall to their knees with gratitude. It was like no one ever told them *what* made them special, or *why* they were valued. Later, they'd tell us how their ability to show (and receive) appreciation was saving their relationships and hitting home with their kids. Their teamwork improved, as well as their self-esteem and success on the job.

In his timeless book, *How to Win Friends and Influence People*, Mr. Carnegie says, "Let's cease thinking of our accomplishments, our wants. Then forget flattery. Give honest, sincere appreciation. Be 'hearty in your approbation and lavish in your praise,' and people will cherish your words and treasure them and repeat them over a lifetime— repeat them years after you have forgotten them."[3]

If you watch the TV show, *Undercover Boss*, you'll notice there are tears in almost every episode. When the boss reveals their identity and salutes the employees' efforts, both of them will typically start to cry. That's when I get weepy, too. That show reminds me how difficult people's lives can be and how much recognition matters.

Part of the problem, I believe, is that no one teaches us how to give meaningful compliments. We say things like "good job" or "way to go," which offer encouragement, but they don't tell the person what they did well. Brief validation still makes a difference, though. There was a gentleman at one of my trainings who saved a Post-it® note from his boss. I asked, "What did it say?" "Great job," he replied. "For what?" He said, "I have no idea, but to me, this is gold!"

If you have trouble giving compliments, you're not alone. Negative words are often more accessible, yet these critical thoughts won't lead to kindness. With Step 4, you'll train your mind to see the positive in each person. You'll learn how to "phrase your praise," so it doesn't sound awkward or creepy.

Let's talk about why we are resistant to giving compliments. When I work with someone who is resistant to giving appreciation, they are often unhappy with own their lives or jobs. They can't find the good in others because they can't find it within their situation. That's why Steps 1-3 of the Kindness Habit were designed to get you in an optimistic frame of mind. Your brain will be flushed with feel-good chemicals, and that will affect how you see yourself and others.

Showing appreciation can be a challenge if it wasn't modeled in your upbringing and it's rarely done at your office. I often see salespeople transfer to management positions without understanding how to motivate their teams. Once, I coached a manager who led 600 people and had received zero leadership training. When these clients find me, I can't wait to tell them, "Your influence is about to drastically improve."

Another reason we're losing the ability to express appreciation is on account of social media. With one click, you can wish someone a generic happy birthday or congratulatory sentiment. While your gesture may be kind, your greeting has no emotional power. Those who make *thoughtful* comments online and send handwritten cards provide something that's meaningful to the receiver. A few extra minutes of consideration can make a lasting memory and reinforce a relationship.

Anyone can get validation on dating apps, through social media, and in chat rooms, and when a person you love doesn't feel like they are loved, they might be tempted to outsource appreciation online. It's an easy place to go for quick attention. Steps 1-3 will help you sense when your family or partner needs your affection. There's no question that your in-person gesture of kindness will trump a favored tweet.

Because an email or text conveys *instant* appreciation, we tend to choose it over handwritten notes or cards. If I look at the holiday greetings I've received over the years, they're a fraction of what they used to be. The same is true for birthday and thank you cards. At the post office, I saw a cardboard display saying, "Fill their mailboxes, not the inboxes." Since you know how good it feels to receive cards in the mail, commit to being a person who does it regularly.

If you practice Steps 1-3, it won't feel unnatural to take **Step 4: Appreciate one person each day**. Your kindness will arise as an inspired idea that generates good vibes. You might be afraid, however, of sounding cheesy or being inappropriate. It's important to name these fears and conquer them. We'll address this later in the chapter.

What you might not realize is everyone wants to be appreciated differently. Some people feel horrified when they're praised in public. Others love it. Some people want gifts of thanks while others want vacation time or to get a hug. When showing appreciation, it's important to consider how the receiver likes to be honored. We tend to give in the ways that *we* like to receive. Your appreciation will make a bigger impact if it's customized to the preferences of the person. For instance, a group of us were buying a gift for a woman from the National Speakers Association who went above and beyond for our leadership committee. We all thought she'd like a day at the spa. Turns out, she loves ballroom dancing. We wound up writing a check to her instructor.

In "The Five Languages of Appreciation in the Workplace: Empowering Organizations by Encouraging People," authors Gary Chapman and Paul White offer a series of compelling statistics. They say, "51% of managers believe they do a good job of appreciating, while just 17% of their employees said they felt appreciated." They also mention two surveys. The *Chicago Tribune* concluded the number one reason people enjoy their work is because they feel appreciated. Add to that, *Business News Daily*'s data: 80% of employees said they feel motivated to give more when their boss shows appreciation. More than half of those respondents said they would stay longer in the company if they felt more appreciated.[4] These findings indicate what I've witnessed over the span of my career—people leave jobs because of the managers, not the position, salary, nor company.

When I help businesses develop appreciation programs, they gradually notice a marked decrease in turnover and sick time. When they add up the cost of hiring, firing, recruiting, and replacing employees as well as the cost of health insurance, the totals are astronomical. Appreciation secures loyalty within teams and creates a wave of healthy energy that ultimately improves sales and the customers' experience. Stephen R. Covey explains this perfectly, "Always treat your employees exactly as you want them to treat your best customers."[5]

Another reason we don't compliment? Because it's common to reject praise. Have you ever liked someone's sweater and they said, "This old thing? $5.99 at Goodwill."? Women are notorious for deflecting compliments, and men can be self-deprecating, too. Next time you're acknowledged, don't try to be humble. All you have to do is smile and say, "Thanks."

I've heard that children who misbehave are often screaming for love and appreciation. When they feel secure at school and in their family, their choices will get better. We sometimes fail to offer praise because the behavior that needs changed seems more important. This also happens when training dogs. Screaming won't stop them from barking or scratching at the door. It takes a few tasty treats and a sweet tone of voice for the dog to comply.

Psychologist Henry H. Goddard conducted a study on energy levels in children using an instrument called the ergograph. He discovered that when tired children were given a word of praise or approval, the ergograph showed an upward surge of energy in the kids. When they were criticized or discouraged, the ergograph showed their physical energy had taken a sudden nosedive.[6] The same dynamic occurs in adults. If I'm jogging up a hill and somebody smiles or gives a thumbs up, it'll give me jolt of energy. This is why supporters line the roads during races. Those cheers of encouragement carry participants through those final, grueling miles.

The same dynamic happens in professional settings. Appreciation energizes people in the workplace better than any caffeinated beverage. It also builds confidence to apply for promotions or to ask for a raise. When you're told what you do well, you can sell your strengths with complete assurance. When you know what makes you unique, competition isn't as scary. Your self-esteem will also give assurance to anyone who is hiring you.

One final reason leaders don't give appreciation is because they're tired. It can be lonely at the top. They have to hear complaints all day and find ways to fix them. They give encouragement and almost never get any in return. With several of my clients, I've had employees tell their owners and presidents what they appreciated about them. Years later, many of those company leaders say they *still* have those letters, so they can be reminded of the good they've done.

Have you ever saved a handwritten card or note? Why? Because it's evidence of your connection to a person and the interactions that you've shared. It's something you can hold and treasure. Plus, handwriting sends a message about your personality. Appreciation can be expressed in a variety of ways, but whenever possible, choose to send a handwritten item. You never know when it will become a keepsake for someone who needs to hear a kind word.

Now, let's discuss how to give proper appreciation.

1. WHAT DO YOU ADMIRE ABOUT THEM?

In my corporate trainings, I ask people to go around the room and say what they admire about each person. They are asked to give specific examples:

- Joe, I love your dedication to projects. You never let us down.
- Susan, your patience with difficult clients is unwavering. Thank you!
- Andy, you're always on time for meetings, and it helps us stay on track.

Afterwards, people will confide in me and say, "I never knew others saw me that way." That's because we tend to remember negative words from the past, and we don't give ourselves credit from the things we do well. The Kindness Habit is created to lift the fog, so you can see your own strengths and be able to recognize them in others.

2. BE SPECIFIC

When giving appreciation, it has to be customized. Like the examples listed above, people need specifics on what they've done well and what differentiates them. You can't just say, "You're awesome," you have to describe *why* you think they're awesome in order to have a bigger impact.

Here are examples of specific compliments:
- You are one of the most generous people I've ever met.
- I can always count on you to pick up the phone.
- Your laugh makes everyone smile.
- Our talks give me clarity about what to do next.
- You always take time to listen.
- The way you closed that client was creative and bold.
- I can always rely on you to follow through.
- Your financial advice has saved us thousands of dollars.

Sure, it takes time to come up with these statements, but just think of the impact. This is how you reward and reinforce what's good in others. It also demonstrates to everyone around you what it looks, sounds, and feels like to give a first-class compliment.

3. BE SINCERE

A Buddhist monk said, "Words have the power to both destroy and heal. When words are both true and kind, they can change our world."[7] Sincerity comes from the heart and needs no reply. Flattery comes from a selfish intention, and it hopes for a desired result. To access sincerity, notice who has been catching your eye, who has been in your thoughts, and who nearby could use a dose of kindness.

- Do you see a gorgeous pair of shoes on a stranger? Let them know!
- Are you wondering how a friend's been feeling? Check on them.
- Did you like what a friend wrote in their blog? Leave a nice comment.
- Had a fabulous meal? Tell the manager or write an online review.

It's fun to point out what people are doing well. Sometimes, your compliment will catch them off guard, and they'll learn something new about themselves. When you search for good in the world, it's truly amazing who and what you can find.

4. GIVE PRAISE TO EVERYONE

One of my long-term clients is a car dealer in Southwest Washington. When we started, I interviewed staff at every level of the business, which led to a startling discovery. Most of the time, they told me, the sales department received all the praise.

This launched a company-wide appreciation program, called "Believe in Nice." Each month, one person wins $200 for a charity of their choice and $200 to use on their own. They also get a primo parking spot, lunch with the owners, and their picture in the dealership newsletter. Sometimes, a finance person will win. Other times, it's a technician, lot attendant, or someone in the IT department or human resources that wins. Everyone adds to the success of a business.

For another client's store opening, we created photo profiles of every associate and listed their favorite movies, books, foods, and vacations. This helped people learn each other's names and engage based on mutual interests. While visiting another client, I noticed bare walls in the breakroom with only a picture of the manager. I suggested they replace it ASAP with team member photos and fun facts about each person. People want to be part of a community and feel like they have a purpose at work.

Whether you're at work or roaming around town, remember to spread your kindness to people of all races, genders, ages, and vocations. Ask yourself, "Who haven't I properly acknowledged or taken the time to get to know?" Then, make a point to do so.

5. KEEP IT CLASSY

With sexual harassment suits being filed every day, people have become cautious and even fearful of being inappropriate. This is a positive movement for our culture because it's raising awareness and opening important dialogue, but I fear it will squelch the flow of compliments. Let's get clear about what's going to get you in trouble.

At work, you cannot comment on a person's looks. You can say, "Gina, your positive energy is appreciated," but you cannot say, "Gina, it looks like you lost weight." It's best to focus on a thing—their watch, glasses, shoes, purse, coffee mug, or jewelry. These items are safe.

Then, you can look at their accomplishments. What have they demonstrated?

- Congrats on getting record donations for the food bank.

- Congrats on hitting your fourth quarter goals.
- Congrats on your first 90 days at the job.
- Congrats on the start of your new podcast.
- Congrats on completing the 5K race.
- Congrats on the birth of your child.

If you're a male coworker, you shouldn't tell Mary she looks great in that dress. If you're Mary's friend or partner, you most definitely can. Woman-to-woman compliments have very few limits. Cross-gender comments require discernment. Regardless, you'll be safe if you focus on a person's character and accomplishments, not their looks.

6. MAKE APPRECIATION A DAILY EVENT

Annual reviews can be a waste of time if that's the only assessment tool that's used. You should be constantly giving feedback to your team—quarterly, monthly, weekly, daily, and in the moment. When I played volleyball in high school and college, we were coached at practice, during the game, and afterwards. Whether you're taking a new class or you've hired a coach or trainer, part of your success depends on the quality and *consistency* of the feedback you receive. Appreciation works the same way. It's how winning teams are built and individuals continue to improve.

Consistent appreciation is also how you keep volunteers happy. For years, I've been an active volunteer for the Children's Cancer Association. Each time I perform any kind of service for them, they send a handwritten thank you note signed by everyone in the office. I'm loyal to CCA, partially because of the way they treat me. When you appreciate nonprofit volunteers, it keeps them involved in the mission and gives them a sense of belonging.

When showing appreciation, brevity is fine. You can reach out and simply say, "Thinking of you." That's all that's needed. You can put a note on your neighbor's windshield that says, "Have a great day!" You can send articles to clients, "Thought you'd like this." No other words are necessary, and your kindness will be noted.

If you're on LinkedIn, recognize people's work anniversaries. Congratulate them on their recent accomplishment or for being dedicated to their jobs. I've found that almost everyone knows the date they began their job. It's kind to let people know their presence and efforts have been noticed. In the workplace, you can celebrate work anniversaries with a cake or a gift card or swing by their office to say thank you.

Finally, if you're the recipient of a kind deed, acknowledge that it was received and appreciated. I think we all have wondered if a package or delivery arrived because there was no email, text, phone call, or thank you note to tell us. Be the kind of person who says, "Thank you." It seems like common sense, yet this common courtesy is often ignored.

Kindness comes in many forms. Here are a few ideas to "appreciate" both silently and "out loud":

AT WORK:
- Say please and thank you
- Thank janitors and cleaning crew
- Bring food to celebrate events
- Give thumbs up, high fives, and fist bumps
- Write customers a thank you
- Give an employee an extra vacation day
- Write a LinkedIn review

- Compliment a coworker in a group email
- Use people's names when talking to them

IN THE COMMUNITY:
- Fill out surveys when asked
- Rate your driver on Uber and Lyft
- Thank people who clean public bathrooms
- Leave a note and a snack for the mail carrier
- Compliment people on their cars and yards
- Acknowledge people's pets
- Smile and wave to drivers when they're courteous
- Compliment the manager or clerk at a store
- Ask how service workers are doing and then listen

AT HOME:
- Write loving messages on the bathroom mirror with dry-erase markers
- Comment when someone gets a haircut or makes any kind of change
- Stick a Post-it note in the car with an encouraging message
- Celebrate milestones and achievements
- Ask how their day was and then listen
- Surprise them with a favorite meal
- Hide a small gift in their suitcase when they travel
- Tuck a fun note in their lunch bag
- Say *why* you love and appreciate them

Eventually, the Kindness Habit will become part of your routine. This will ensure daily kindness to yourself and others. If you're feeling lonely or lethargic, you'll know how to find happiness and camaraderie with Steps 1-4.

It's said that "Kindness is a language the blind can see and the deaf can hear." So rest assured, your words and actions make a difference with *everyone*. Step 5 invites you to realize the tremendous impact your kindness can have. This final reinforcement is what turns your kindness into an everyday habit.

REMEMBER YOUR POSITIVE IMPACT ON OTHERS

Did you have a coach, teacher, relative, or friend who saw something in you that others did not? Write down <u>three people</u> who have positively influenced your life.

1. What did they do or say to make you feel valued?
2. How did their words or actions cause you to feel?
3. What did you do differently because of them?

It was fifth grade when I joined the Colorado Children's Chorale, led by an award-winning conductor, Duain Wolfe. Our songs went beyond childhood classics. They had complicated rounds and multiple versus, and we even performed once at Lincoln Center in New York.

Duain was a big influence on me for his stage presence alone. I knew it was an honor to be learning from a professional of his caliber. He taught me how to sing from my diaphragm, take care of my throat, and become a performer, which meant faking a smile when needed. Through his leadership, it also became sealed in my mind that practice and rehearsals were the keys to confidence.

My school teacher, Peggy Ballengee, was overjoyed to have three girls in her class who were part of the Chorale. Throughout the year, she would ask us to stand up and sing a few tunes, which she would wildly appreciate. The boys would roll their eyes, but Heidi Vancil, Heidi Anderson, and I would rise to the occasion, sometimes with matching pigtails and ribbons. Mrs. Ballengee didn't know it at the time, but her encouragement would continue to affect me as a woman. Her reassurance told me that my enthusiasm and talents could lighten up a room. This early validation planted seeds for my career and overall future.

Step 5: Remember your positive impact on others.

When you become intentional about kindness, you have the chance to radically improve someone's day—and maybe even their life.

Some people find that statement hard to believe. They doubt if their good deeds are noticed or if their smile is really contagious. If you find yourself in a doubtful place, here's how to take Step 5 and be *certain* your impact has made a difference.

To see your actions in more positive light, you have to know what you naturally do well. What's cool about you? I know a woman who was an outstanding lacrosse player in high school. Today, she volunteers as a referee for a girls lacrosse team. Because of her passion and expertise, she knows she's having an impact not only on the girls but also on the coaches, parents, and possibly the other refs.

Kindness can seem effortless if you start where it's easy.

- If your garden is booming, share your produce.
- If you play an instrument, teach someone who wants to learn.

- If you're a golf or basketball enthusiast, plan an outing with coworkers.
- If you love to cook, bring food to work.
- If you take great pictures, volunteer to photograph an event.
- If you love being creative, offer to make logos or signs when needed.
- If you have a cute pet, take them to work or a retirement center.

Millions of people have used CliftonStrengths to identify their unique talents. This assessment helps you figure out how you'll function best as a person and professional. The test can be taken online, and further information can be found in their books. In *StrengthsFinders 2.0*, author Tom Rath says, "People who do have the opportunity to focus on their strengths every day are six times as likely to be engaged in their jobs and more than three times as likely to report having an excellent quality of life."[1]

When you know your strengths, you'll know where it's natural for you to give back or pay it forward. You'll be able to take **Step 5: Remember your positive impact on others**—and know that it's true!

Step 5 completes the kindness cycle, which starts by giving kindness to yourself, then gives it to others and circles back to you with a reminder of the potency that's at play. You may never know the value of your good deeds, but you can always keep in mind—kindness has been known to save marriages, friendships, lives, careers, and communities. What further proof do you need?

To remember what's good about you, jot down what makes you feel grateful each day. This will give you signs for where to place your kindness. For instance, you might say, "Today, I am grateful for the warmth of my home, the people who care about me, and the food I get to eat."

- Let the warmth of your home lead you to a homeless shelter website to see what they need donated.

- Let your caring company lead you to put away technology and go for walk with a friend, family member, or dog.

- Let your appreciation of foods lead you to organize a food drive or potluck at your company.

Another form of kindness is to keep recipes and family customs alive. When my daughters' grandmother died, they kept grandma's recipe box as a keepsake. At Thanksgiving, we made Shirley's cranberry bread and molasses cookies, like she would have done. I bet Shirley never realized her legacy in the kitchen would affect generations to come. We honor our ancestors when we recreate their dishes and desserts each year.

Is there a food that everyone associates with you? Maybe you make a mean lasagna, or you're known for your apple pie or clever BBQ technique. Realize the importance of food in our lives. It carries nourishment, memories, and emotional support.

In my daily acts of kindness, I continue to be reminded that everyone has times when they're grieving a loss, devastated by a diagnosis, or struggling at work or home. These people need your kindness. You never know what's happening with someone when you pass them on the streets. They could be leaving a funeral, ending a relationship, or suffering from the flu.

Never underestimate your kind deeds, even if people don't smile or wave back. To someone who's in trauma or grief, your kindness could keep them afloat when it feels like they're sinking. Philosopher Cornel West said, "Empathy is not simply a matter of trying to imagine what others are going through, but having the will to muster enough courage to do something about it."[2] Everyone can do *something* to make someone's life better.

Best-selling author L.R. Knost suggests a way to bring kindness to humanity. "Do not be dismayed by the brokenness of the world. All things break. And all things can be mended. Not with time, as they say, but with intention. So go. Love intentionally, extravagantly, unconditionally. The broken world waits in the darkness for the light that is you."[3]

On social media, you'll see people whose lives appear to be flawless, yet behind the scenes, they have dramas like the rest of us. They might appear to have it all—family, friends, health, wealth, and travel—yet *no one* is exempt from life's ups and downs. Remember that people need your *in person* kindness more than your online support. You might question your friend's "Fakebook" profile, but do not ignore them in real life. Those who get lots of attention online, and those who don't, are often lonely. Have your kindness be tangible!

- Did they accomplish a big goal? Ask them to lunch to celebrate.
- Are they leaving for vacation? Call to wish them well.
- Did they receive hundreds of birthday wishes online? Say it to their face.

Do you remember Susan Boyle, the singer from the TV show, *Britain's Got Talent*? She was an average, older woman who would otherwise blend into a crowd, but because she had the courage to sing, people showered her with appreciation and feedback that confirmed she was indeed talented. The same is true for almost any contestant on *American Idol* or *The Voice*. They all need someone to confirm their potential and bring it out in them. I think about those I have coached who have taken on bigger roles in companies. All they needed were a few small changes and a trusted person to say, "You can do this!" You'd be shocked at how many people have never received encouragement or been told what's great about themselves.

The inability to see our own brilliance reminds me of the *Wizard of Oz*. Each character wanted something they thought they didn't have—brains, heart, courage, and home. In the end, the gifts they wanted to receive were within their grasp all along. All Dorothy had to do was feel grateful and recite, "There's no place like home." The Good Witch could be renamed the Queen of Kindness. Because of her smile and good deeds, she was loved by everyone over the rainbow. In the end, she reminded each character of their distinctive powers. You can do the same for everyone in your life.

If you can't find the energy to "appreciate out loud," you can make a positive impact by being a good listener. I cannot stress enough how badly this is needed, especially in business. We get distracted while talking on the phone and get sidetracked by our thoughts and technology while we're listening to someone in person. It's a high form of appreciation to listen well and have the speaker feel heard.

Here are 10 actions to improve your listening skills:

1. Stop. Drop. Goal – Stop what you're doing, drop what's distracting, and achieve your goal of being an attentive listener.

2. Choose your environment – Find the best place to have a conversation. Consider privacy and sound levels.

3. Look at the speaker – Your eye contact will indicate that you're with them 100%.

4. Turn off your thoughts – Put your worries aside and practice being present. Concentrate on the speaker's words.

5. Use open body language – Uncross your arms and legs. This will put the speaker at ease, so they can keep talking.

6. Reinforce words and messages when appropriate – "What I heard you say was we're moving forward with the project on Monday."

7. Ask open ended questions – "Tell me more about that." "What was the highlight of your weekend?" These will elicit more than a yes or no.

8. Train your eyes to see nonverbal signs – Look for signs of discomfort—fidgeting, looking at their phone, or turning away.

9. Be patient – Let the other person finish their comment before you formulate your response and speak.

10. Remember your impact – Your time and attention is what people will remember after you're gone.

When a celebrity or musician dies, it's touching to read what people say about them. I often think, why did it take their death to hear how much they meant? So often, we keep our kind thoughts inside until there's a funeral. At that point, the person they were meant for can no longer hear them. Speak words of gratitude now, so you don't have regrets.

Pericles said, "What you leave behind is not what is engraved in stone monuments, but what is woven into the lives of others."[4] When your time comes, people won't talk about your cars, houses, watches, or clothes. They'll talk about how you made their lives better. The American Cancer Society reports, "In the U.S, approximately 41 out of 100 men and 38 out of 100 women will develop cancer."[5] Let's all accept the fragility of life and take advantage of the time we've been given. There's no time to waste!

One of the most popular memes I've ever shared was strangely succinct: "Be known for your kindness and grace." The simplicity of it is appealing, and it seems like an attainable goal, but only if you're willing to make it intentional.

Ellen DeGeneres has become known as an ambassador of kindness. This earned her the Presidential Medal of Freedom and a record-breaking 20 People's Choice Awards. In one of her acceptance speeches, she famously said, "It's a little strange to actually get an award for being nice and generous and kind, which is what we're all supposed to do with one another. That's the point of being human." In Ellen's "One Million Acts of Good" campaign, people submitted photos and stories from their kind deeds. Those can be found with the hashtag, #GoodGoesAround, and can serve as an endless source of inspiration.[6]

Country music star Tim McGraw adds his influence with the song, "Humble and Kind." If you look up this video on YouTube, you'll see people around the world who are giving kindness and also in need of it. In the chorus, he sings,

"Hold the door, say please, say thank you,
don't steal, don't cheat, and don't lie.
I know you got mountains to climb,
but always stay humble and kind."[7]

Being kind makes you feel good, but the effect it can have on someone's life is mind-blowing. People need kindness, now more than ever. Whether they've spilled their coffee or lost a loved one, the smallest gestures could have a ripple effect that never ends. You can be the one to start it with a smile, compliment, phone call, or hug. Now that you know how to maximize your happiness and impact with the Kindness Habit, get ready for the incredible changes it will evoke:

REDUCE: Stress, anger, loneliness, turnover, apathy, and depression

IMPROVE: Attitude, productivity, creativity, relationships, and bottom line

Any habit you want to stick takes effort and persistence. They say practice makes perfect, but the Kindness Habit isn't meant to be perfected. It's meant to be *practiced* for the rest of your life. Practice makes permanent. With Steps 1-3, you will fine-tune your awareness and take charge of your happiness. With Step 4, you'll grow your ability to appreciate, and with Step 5, you'll remember why all of this matters.

Relationship expert Dr. Matt Townsend summarizes this nicely, "One smile can start a friendship. One word can end a fight. One look can save a relationship. One person can change your life."[8]

Now, it's your turn.

You can and will make a difference.

25 ACTS OF KINDNESS THAT CELEBRATE HUMAN LIFE:

1. Offer assistance to elderly and disabled people at the store.

2. Give up your seat to a vet or family who wants to sit together on the plane.

3. Help a neighbor rake leaves, cut grass, trim weeds, or shovel snow.

4. Stay 10 minutes extra to help a coworker finish a task.

5. Send a card for no reason.

6. Notify someone of empty toilet paper rolls in bathrooms.

7. Tell a person if their zipper is down or there's food in their teeth.

8. Hold open doors and elevators for people.

9. Offer to help with luggage or heavy bags at the airport.

10. When paying bills, add a fun message to the memo or envelope.

11. Let people in front of you in traffic.

12. Give blood or become an organ donor.

13. Tape cash to a vending machine to surprise the next person.

14. Acknowledge new employees at work.

15. Volunteer for a nonprofit organization.

16. Turn off technology and be present.

17. Help people clean up spills.

18. Assist when someone falls down.

19. Donate clothes to shelters and needy families.

20. Feed the parking meter for someone.

21. If you feel safe, help someone change a tire or jump their car battery.

22. Pick up trash when you see it in public.

23. Leave a generous tip or a positive rating.

24. Write endorsements and testimonials.

25. Hold a kindness party where everyone tells stories of kindness in their life.

Introduction

1. "Unexpected kindness is the most powerful . . . ," goodreads, accessed January 13, 2018, https://www. goodreads.com/quotes/867830-unexpected-kindness-is-the-most-powerful-least-costly-and-most.

2. "The deepest craving in human nature . . . ," QuotesEverlasting.com, accessed January 13, 2018, http:// quoteseverlasting.com/author.php?a=William%20James.

3. Scott Bernard Nelson, "2013 Top Workplaces: Great employers, happy employees," OregonLive, September 12, 2013, http://www.oregonlive.com/business/index. ssf/2013/09/great_employers_happy_employee.html.

4. Erin Donley, "Best Smile in Oregon," HuffPost, February 22, 2015, https://www.huffingtonpost.com/entry/best-smile-in-portland-or_b_6518646.html.

5. Janet Choi, "How to Boost Productivity: Autonomy, Mastery, and Purpose," Delivering Happiness, October 11, 2017, http://blog.deliveringhappiness.com/the-motivation-trifecta-autonomy-mastery-and-purpose.

6. "Act as if what you do makes a difference . . . ," QuotesEverlasting.com, accessed January 13, 2018, http:// quoteseverlasting.com/author.php?a=William%20James.

Step 1: Stop Your Daily Routine

1. Ashley Halsey III, "Distracted driving: 9 die, 1,060 hurt each day, CDC says," *Washington Post: Gridlock*, February 24, 2014, https://www.washingtonpost.com/news/dr-gridlock/ wp/2014/02/24/distracted-driving-9-die-1060-hurt-each-day-cdc-says/?utm_term=.ad80a0f233ed.

2. Neuroskeptic, "The 70,000 Thoughts Per Day Myth?" *Discover Magazine: Blogs*, May 9, 2012, http://blogs. discovermagazine.com/neuroskeptic/2012/05/09/the-70000-thoughts-per-day-myth/#.Wlp5tzdG200.

3. Ralph Marston, "Giving," *The Daily Motivator*, November 23, 2017, http://greatday.com/motivate/171123.html.

4. Maggie Jackson, "Maggie Jackson speaks at LO Advertising Conference 2016," filmed February 29, 2016 at Local Online Advertising Conference – 2016, New York, NY, Maggie Jackson, video, 3:55, http://maggie-jackson. com/media.

5. Thom Shanker and Matt Richtel, "In New Military, Data Overload Can Be Deadly," *New York Times*, January 16, 2011 http://www.nytimes.com/2011/01/17/technology/17brain. html?pagewanted=all.

6. Matt Richtel, *Deadly Wandering* (New York: Harper Collins, 2014), 219.

7. "Scary Ways Technology Affects Your Sleep," National Sleep Foundation, accessed January 13, 2018, https://sleep. org/articles/ways-technology-affects-sleep/.

8. Richard Feloni, "A retired Navy SEAL commander who wakes up at 4:30 a.m. shares his morning routine," Business Insider, November 13, 2017, http://www.businessinsider.com/ retired-navy-seal-jocko-willink-morning-routine-2017-11.

9. Admiral William H. McRaven, *Make Your Bed: Little Things That Can Change Your Life . . . And Maybe the World*, (New York: Grand Central Publishing, 2017).

10. Roman Krznaric, "How We Ruined Mindfulness," *Time*, May 26, 2017, http://time.com/4792596/mindfulness-exercises-morality-carpe-diem/.

11. Robert Klemko, "SI's 2017 Sportsperson of the Year: He Isn't on the Field, but J.J. Watt Is Still Lifting Houston up,"

Sports Illustrated, December 5, 2017, https://www.si.com/ sportsperson/2017/12/05/si-sportsperson-of-the-year-jj-watt-houston-texans.

Step 2: Look up and notice your surroundings

1. Charles Duhigg, *Power of Habit*, (New York: Random House, 2014).

2. "Stress is caused by being here, but wanting . . . ," AZquotes, accessed on January 13, 2018, http://www. azquotes.com/quote/578687.

3. Suzanne Carbone, "Look up from your iDevices and notice the world," *Sydney Morning Herald,* May 10, 2014, http://www.smh.com.au/digital-life/mobiles/look-up-from-your-idevices-and-notice-the-world-20140508-zr6wh.html.

4. Prince Ea, "Can We Auto-Correct Humanity," YouTube, September 29, 2014, video, 3:27, https://www.youtube.com/ watch?v=dRl8EIhrQjQ.

5. Naima Montacer, "Nature's Medicine: The Health Benefits of Being Outdoors," *Earth911*, July 19, 2017, https:// earth911.com/living-well-being/health-benefits-outdoors/.

6. "Distracted Driving," National Highway Traffic Safety Administration, accessed January 13, 2018, https://www. nhtsa.gov/risky-driving/distracted-driving.

7. Maureen McGrath, "No Sex Marriage – Masturbation, Loneliness, Cheating and Shame," filmed May 28, 2016 at TEDxStanleyPark, Vancouver, B.C., Canada, YouTube, video, 21:52, https://www.youtube.com/ watch?v=LVgzOyHVcj4.

8. Stephen R. Covey, *The 7 Habits of Highly Effective People: Powerful Lessons in Personal Change*, (Massachusetts and Washington D.C.: Free Press, 1989).

9. Maria Popova, "Simone Weil on Attention and Grace," brainpickings, accessed January 13, 2018, https://www.brainpickings.org/2015/08/19/simone-weil-attention-gravity-and-grace/.

10. Gary Turk, "Look Up," YouTube, April 25, 2014, video, 4:58, https://www.youtube.com/watch?v=Z7dLU6fk9QY.

Step 3: Smile and take a deep breath

1. "We shall never know . . . ," BrainyQuote, accessed January 13, 2018, https://www.brainyquote.com/quotes/mother_teresa_125711.

2. Richard Kehl, *Breathing on Your Own: Quotations for Independent Thinkers*, (Seattle: Darling & Company, 2001), 121.

3. Leo Ridrich, "The Science of Smiling: A Guide to the World's Most Powerful Gesture," Buffer Social, April 9, 2013, https://blog.bufferapp.com/the-science-of-smiling-a-guide-to-humans-most-powerful-gesture.

4. Darryl Davis, "#SmileDOSE #KeepSmiling," Facebook, December 8, 2017, https://www.facebook.com/darrylspeaks/photos/a.10151036621908917.457145.197118118916/10155907633178917.

5. Darryl Davis, *How to Design a Life Worth Smiling About*, (New York: McGraw Hill Education Books, 2014).

6. Harvard Business Review, "A Face to Face Request is 34 Times More Successful Than an Email," Psychological Science, April 12, 2017, https://www.psychologicalscience.org/news/a-face-to-face-request-is-34-times-more-successful-than-an-email.html.

7. Roger E. Axtell, *Gestures, the Do's and Taboos of Body Language Around the World*, (Hoboken, NJ: Wiley, 1991), 17.

8. Davis, *How to Design a Life Worth Smiling About.*

9. Amy Cuddy, "Your Body Language May Shape Who You Are," filmed June 28, 2012 at TEDGlobal, Edinburgh, TEDx, video, 20:56, https://www.ted.com/talks/amy_cuddy_your_body_language_shapes_who_you_are.

10. Julie, "Mindful Mondays: William Saroyan (and Earnest Hemingway)," Making Mindfulness, February 17, 2014, http://www.makingmindfulness.com/2014/02/mindful-mondays-william-saroyan-and-ernest-hemingway/.

11. Judy E. Davidson, Patricia G. Graham, Lori Montross-Thomas, William A. Norcross, and Giovanna Zerbi, "Code Lavender: Cultivating Intentional Acts of Kindness in Response to Stressful Work Situations," *EXPLORE: The Journal of Science and Healing* 13, (April 2017), ResearchGate, https://www.researchgate.net/publication/316087481_Code_Lavender_Cultivating_Intentional_Acts_of_Kindness_in_Response_to_Stressful_Work_Situations.

Step 4: Appreciate one person each day

1. Denice Lee Yohn, "Delivering Happiness: Company Mission and Community Movement," *Forbes*, January 27, 2016, https://www.forbes.com/sites/deniselyohn/2016/01/27/delivering-happiness-company-mission-and-community-movement/#20ed9f453467.

2. Dale Carnegie, *How to Win Friends and Influence People*, (New York: Simon & Schuster, 2009), 51.

3. Carnegie, *How to Win Friends and Influence People*, 32.

4. Greg Thornburg, "The Five Languages of Appreciation in the Workplace: Empowering Organizations by Encouraging People," PowerPoint, University of Arkansas Community College, Batesville, AR, accessed January 13, 2018, aasfaa.net/Portals/6/Documents/2017/Five-Languages.pptx.

5. Covey, *7 Habits of Highly Effective People: Powerful Lessons in Personal Change*, 58.

6. John C. Maxwell, *25 Ways to Win with People: How to Make Others Feel Like a Million Bucks,* (Nashville: Thomas Nelson, Inc., 2005), 14.

7. Jack Kornfield, *Buddha's Little Instruction Book*, (New York: Bantam Books, 1994), 5.

Step 5: Remember your positive impact on others

1. Tom Rath, *StrengthsFinders 2.0*, (New York: Gallup Press, 2007), iii.

2. "Empathy is not simply a matter of . . . ," goodreads, accessed January 13, 2018, https://www.goodreads.com/author/quotes/6176.Cornel_West.

3. L. R. Knost, "Do not be dismayed by the brokenness . . . ," My Soul in Silence Waits, July 8, 2017, https://insilencewaits.wordpress.com/2017/07/08/i-just-want-to-do-love-right/.

4. "What you leave behind is not . . . ," QuotesValley.com, accessed January 13, 2018, http://www.quotesvalley.com/what-you-leave-behind-is-not-what-is-engraved-in-stone-monuments-but-what-is-woven-into-the-lives-of-others-5/.

5. American Cancer Society, "Cancer Facts & Figures 2017," (Atlanta: American Cancer Society, 2017), 2, annual report, https://www.cancer.org/content/dam/cancer-org/research/cancer-facts-and-statistics/annual-cancer-facts-and-figures/2017/cancer-facts-and-figures-2017.pdf.

6. Naja Rayne, "Watch Ellen DeGeneres Be Hilarious Yet Touching Accepting the People's Choice Award for Favorite Humanitarian," *People*, January 7, 2016, http://people.com/awards/ellen-degeneres-hilariously-accepts-favorite-humanitarian-award/.

7. Tim McGraw, "Humble and Kind," YouTube, January 21, 2016, video, 4:29, https://www.youtube.com/watch?v=awzNHuGqoMc.

8. "One smile can start a friendship . . . ," Matt Townsend, accessed January 13, 2018, http://matttownsend.com/.

ABOUT THE AUTHOR

For over half of her life, Allison Clarke, CSP, has been solving communication problems for companies and teaching the power of kindness. She's helped professionals around the globe to break through barriers and get results that improve their productivity, profitability, and personal happiness.

As a "Top 25 Master Trainer" for Dale Carnegie Corporation, Allison spent 16 years witnessing miraculous transformations. This gave her the foundation needed to launch Allison Clarke Consulting. Her client list includes Intel, Kroger, Adidas, Dignity Memorial, Niagara Bottling, and Trident Seafoods. These diverse companies have one thing in common—they know the success of their companies depends on their people.

Allison's first book, What Will They Say? 30 Funerals in 60 Days, is a study of leadership and what it means to leave a memorable impact. In The Kindness Habit, she offers concrete steps to leave a legacy of kindness and grace.

Allison was the President of the Oregon National Speakers Association and now serves at the national level. In 2016, she earned the CSP™ (Certified Speaking Professional), a designation that's based on criteria only 12% of speakers worldwide have able to meet. Allison has been a longtime volunteer and Ambassador with Children's Cancer Association. She lives in Portland, Oregon, and has two daughters.

To hire Allison to speak or train your company, visit AllisonClarkeConsulting.com. You're also invited to follow Allison's kind acts and share yours on Facebook at "Kindness Habit." #KindnessHabit